101
WACKY
Computer
Jokes

101 WACKY Computer Jokes

By J.B. & G.C. Stamper

SCHOLASTIC INC.
New York Toronto London Auckland Sydney

No part of this publication may be reproduced in whole or in part, or stored in a retrieval system, or transmitted in any form or by any means, electronic, mechanical, photocopying, recording, or otherwise, without written permission of the publisher. For information regarding permission, write to Scholastic Inc., Attention: Permissions Department, 555 Broadway, New York, NY 10012.

ISBN 0-590-13004-8

12 11 10 9 8 7 6 5 4 3 2 1   8 9/9 0 1 2 3/0
Printed in the U.S.A.
First Scholastic printing, January 1998

Computer Comedy

Where do cool mice live?

In mousepads.

Where do computers go to dance?

The disk-o.

What did the spider do inside the computer?

It made a web page.

What do you get when you cross a mountain goat with a computer?

Lots of RAM.

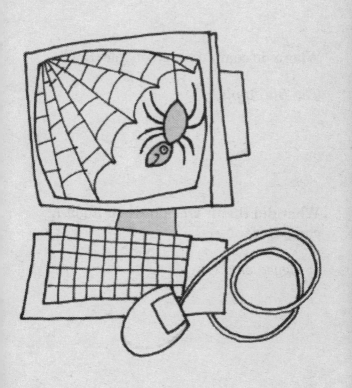

Where do computers go on vacation?

The Big Apple.

What did the fir tree do when it got a computer?

It logged on.

What do you call a computer superhero?

A Screen Saver.

Computer City

Mack: Where do computers go to shop?
Jack: Where?
Mack: The hardware store.

Mack: What did the customers do in the busy computer store?
Jack: What?
Mack: They got on line.

Mack: What makes a good computer salesman?
Jack: I don't know.
Mack: He can drive a hard bargain.

Silly Software

What software helps you lose weight?

Slim City.

What did the rooster whisper?

"My crow soft."

What is Dracula's favorite software?

After Dark.

Why did the witch buy a computer?

She needed spellcheck.

A man and a woman from Sim City got married and had two boys. What were they called?

The Sim sons.

Why should you always use a spellcheck?

So they're know miss steaks in you're righting.

Why was the computer wearing shades?

To cover its Windows.

Sam and Ram

Sam: I bought a new computer in Hawaii.
Ram: What kind is it?
Sam: A Pine-Apple.

Sam: How can you tell your computer is getting old?
Ram: How?
Sam: It loses its memory.

Sam: Did you hear that the zoo has a website?
Ram: Really?
Sam: They're on-lion.

Ram: How do you park a computer?
Sam: I don't know, how?
Ram: You back it up.

How is the Internet like your front yard?

You have to modem both.

What did the astronaut write in his
E-mail?

Sigh . . . brrr . . . Space is cold!

Why did the computer get glasses?

To improve its websight.

What happens if you don't use the
Internet for a while?

Your computer gets cobwebs.

What do you call two websites that get married?

The newlywebs.

Computer Favorites

Favorite Book:

Charlotte's Web Page

Favorite Movie:

RAM-bo

Second Favorite Movie:

Wizard of Dos

Favorite TV show:

The Text-Files

Favorite Rock Group:

The Grateful Disk

What did the boy computer say to the girl computer?

You're the Apple of my eye.

What do computer couples fight about?

Who has to take out the trash.

Where does Spider-Man find a date?

On the World Wide Web.

Knock-knocks

Knock-knock.
Who's there?
Virgil.
Virgil who?
Virgil Reality.

Knock-knock.
Who's there?
Icon.
Icon who?
Icon make you open the door.

Knock-knock.
Who's there?
Kay.
Kay who?
Kay board.

Why can't computers play tennis?

They try to surf the net.

How do you compliment a computer?

"You're looking chipper today!"

What did the shoe salesman do when he got a computer?

He booted up.

What did the prisoner do when he got a computer?

He escaped.

What is an astronaut's favorite place on a computer?

The space bar.

Why did the computer sneeze?

It had a virus.

Why was the computer so angry?

Because it had a chip on its shoulder.

Where do computers go in the winter?

To Hot Spots.

Why can't you trust a computer?

Because it's shift-key.

Mitten: I never get petted anymore.
Rover: Why's that?
Mitten: My owner got a laptop.

What is a bird's favorite computer software?

A Seedy ROM.

Did you hear about the lion that swallowed a computer?

It became a mane frame!

Where do computers take their sick pets?

To the Intervet.

What's another name for a computer virus?

A megabyte parasite.

What's another name for exit?

The flee key.

Who chases computer criminals?

A hacker-tracker.

What do you call a computer science test?

A RAM exam.

Computer: Did you know that computers are smarter than people?
Human: No, I didn't know that.
Computer: See what I mean?

Ted: Last night my computer died.
Ned: What did it die of?
Ted: A terminal illness.

Boy: Mom, have you been using my new computer?
Mother: Yes, how did you know?
Boy: There's Wite-Out on the screen.

Mother Computer scolding PC Junior:

"Wait till your Data gets home!"

First Computer: Do you have any brothers?
Second Computer: No, only transistors.

What do you get when you cross a dog and a computer?

A machine that has a bark worse than its byte.

What do you get when you cross a computer with an icy road?

A hard drive.

What do you get if you cross a computer with an elephant?

Lots of memory.

What do you get if you cross a computer and one million mosquitoes?

A gigabyte!

What do you get if you cross a spider with an earthworm?

A webcrawler.

Daffy Definitions

State-of-the-art computer: one you can't afford.

Floppy: what your wallet is after buying a computer.

Disk crash: the typical computer reaction to an important deadline.

486: IQ necessary to read computer manuals.

Computer Creatures

What did the elf put on the Internet?

A gnome page.

Which one of the Seven Dwarfs was the first to get a computer?

Floppy.

What do you call the small creatures that make the colors on a computer screen?

Pixelfs.

The Presidents of the Computed States of America

George Washdiskton

Abmodem Lincoln

John Quincy Apples

Warren G. Harddrive

William MouseKinley

Mousetraps

Why were the two mouses arrested?

They were caught drag racing.

What does the President use with his computer in the Oval Office?

A White Mouse.

What do you get with a computer in Alaska?

A moose.

What did the computer say to the mouse?

Your click is my command.

What did the computer trio sing when the lights went out?

Three Blind Mice.

More Knock-knocks

Knock-knock.
Who's there?
Meg.
Meg who?
Meg A. Bytes.

Knock-knock.
Who's there?
Modem.
Modem who?
No modem knock-knocks, please.

Knock-knock.
Who's there?
S.
S. who?
S. Cape while you can.

You Know You've Been Using Your Computer Too Long When:

*you double click the floor button on an elevator.

*you try to push escape to leave a boring class.

*you try to call up a different menu
when your mother serves meatloaf again.

*you try to brighten the monitor when
the sun starts going down.

*you try to delete your little brother.

Cyber-Snacks

What's a computer's favorite snack?

Chips.

Why did the computer cross the road?

To get a byte to eat.

Why did the computer go to the super-market?

To buy its mouse some cheese.

Did you hear about the millionaire kid?

He gave his teacher an Apple and an IBM every day.

What happened to the computer when it crashed?

It got a slipped disk.

What do computers get paid to do?

Net work.

What basketball team is the computer's favorite?

The New Jersey Nets.

Why was the computer kicked out of school?

Because its cursor wouldn't stop.

Why did the boy fail computer class?

Because he didn't know the password.

Where do computers go when they're sad?

Cryberspace.

Why did the Apple lose its memory?

It had a bad case of worms.

The good news is . . . my computer has 80 megabytes.

The bad news is . . . it's hungry!